THE WRETCH ON THE GALLOWS TREE

RHYMES AND CAROLS
BY DANIEL MITSUI

THE WRETCH ON THE GALLOWS TREE

Rhymes and Carols
by Daniel Mitsui

COPYRIGHT © 2024 DANIEL MITSUI

ALL RIGHTS RESERVED

PUBLISHED IN 2024

ISBN: 979-8-9902127-0-1

ILLUSTRATIONS, ORNAMENT, AND TYPEFACES

DRAWN AND DESIGNED BY THE AUTHOR

WWW.DANIELMITSUI.COM

TABLE OF CONTENTS

1. **THE BESOM OF RUIN**
   A SONG OF CONSOLATION

3. **MARY BEARS EMMANUEL**
   A HYMN FOR ADVENT

5. **A CARRACK AND TWO CARAVELS**
   A CAROL FOR ADVENT

7. **THE DEW FALLS**
   A HYMN FOR ADVENT

9. **THE FRUIT OF THY WOMB**
   A HYMN FOR ADVENT

11. **WHEN GOD MADE ADAM**
    A HYMN FOR CHRISTMAS AT MIDNIGHT

14. **GOOD SHEPHERDS**
    A CAROL FOR CHRISTMAS AT MIDNIGHT

16. **A LIGHT SHINES TODAY**
    A BALLADE FOR CHRISTMAS AT DAYBREAK

18. **THE WORD OF GOD**
    A CAROL FOR CHRISTMAS DAY

20. **PURPLE AND PALL**
    A BALLAD ON THE ARA CÆLI

- 23 **THE VIRGIN SANG**
  A CHRISTMAS LULLABY
- 25 **SING NOWELL**
  A CAROL FOR CHRISTMASTIDE
- 27 **NEW YEARS AND AGES**
  A CAROL FOR CIRCUMCISION DAY
- 29 **THE WISEST OF THE WISE**
  A HYMN FOR EPIPHANY
- 32 **THE TREASURES OF THE EARTH**
  A HYMN FOR EPIPHANY
- 36 **JESUS LIVES IN EGYPT**
  A CAROL ON THE FLIGHT INTO EGYPT
- 39 **THE WAY TO BETHLEHEM**
  A CAROL FOR EPIPHANYTIDE
- 41 **GOD IS IN THE TEMPLE AGAIN**
  A CAROL FOR CANDLEMAS
- 43 **VANITAS VANITATUM**
  A SONG ON EARTHLY TRANSIENCE
- 45 **IN THE DESERT**
  A CAROL ON THE TEMPTATION OF JESUS CHRIST
- 47 **MOUNT TABOR**
  A HYMN ON THE TRANSFIGURATION

50   **THE ANGEL'S GREETING**
        A CAROL ON THE ANNUNCIATION

52   **MAIDEN WITHOUT DAPPLE**
        A CAROL ON THE ANNUNCIATION

55   **THY BOSOM FRIEND**
        A CAROL ON THE BETRAYAL OF JESUS CHRIST

57   **COME WAVING BRANCHES**
        A CAROL FOR PALM SUNDAY

59   **BAKÈD BREAD AND WINE SO RED**
        A CAROL FOR MAUNDY THURSDAY

62   **SING WELLAWAY**
        A CAROL ON THE AGONY IN THE GARDEN

64   **THE HEMLOCK**
        A CAROL ON THE DEATH OF JESUS CHRIST

66   **A GODFORSAKEN GOD**
        AN ALPHABET ON THE DEATH OF JESUS CHRIST

70   **NO GREATER LOVE**
        A ROMANCE ON THE DEATH OF JESUS CHRIST

76   **A WRETCH ON A GALLOWS TREE**
        A SONG OF CONSOLATION

79   **BROKEN THINGS**
        A BALLAD FOR THE HOLY TRIDUUM

82 **SEVEN TIMES SEVEN**
   A COUNTING SONG ON THE PASSION

86 **FELIX CULPA**
   A CAROL FOR THE VIGIL OF EASTER

88 **THE SIGN OF JONAH**
   A CAROL FOR EASTER

91 **CHRIST IS RISEN**
   A CAROL FOR EASTER

93 **HE IS NOT DEAD**
   A CAROL FOR EASTER WEEK

96 **EVERY EWE AND RAM**
   A CAROL ON THE GOOD SHEPHERD

99 **ABUNDANT SIGNS AND WONDERS**
   A HYMN ON THE ASCENSION

102 **COME TO THE FEAST**
   A SONG FOR THE DOWNTRODDEN

105 **A GLOSSARY OF UNUSUAL WORDS AND PHRASES**

THE BESOM OF RUIN
A SONG OF CONSOLATION

When thy treasure is strewn by the besom of ruin,
And thy castle is haunted by Reynard and Bruin;
When thy basket and store fall to famine or war,
May thy prayer be the prayer of Hannah.
And the Lord, as sung, will lift thee from dung,
And offer thee water and manna.

When the doom-scales tilt
    to the weight of thy guilt,
A weight like the brick of which Babel was built,
May thy prayer be the prayer
    of the psaltery player
Who cried to his Lord from the deeps.
And the Lord who hears will bottle thy tears,
And shrive a sinner who weeps.

When the Slough of Despond extends beyond
The utmost ends of the mappemond;
When thou cursest the earth
    and the day of thy birth,
May thy prayer be the prayer of Job.
And the Father, for love,
    with the Son and the Dove,
Will make thee a crown and a robe.

When the hellhounds slobber
    at the dance macaber,
May thy prayer be the prayer
    of the right-hand robber.
May it carry thee o'er the heckle-pin moor
And the hair-broad Brig of Dread,
Through Purgatory and into Glory,
At last to rest thy head.

MARY BEARS EMMANUEL
A HYMN FOR ADVENT

On the hallowed ground of Horeb,
Moses saw the bush aflame,
Hid his face and barefoot worshipped,
Heard the Promise and the Name.
    Who can burn but not consume?
    Mary bears Him in her womb.

In the purple Tabernacle
Thirteen rods were put to test.
Lo the tribal staff of Levi
Foliated and floresced.
    Almonds grew on Aaron's Rod;
    Mary bears the Son of God.

In the barley's threshing-circle
Jerubaal wrang out the wool.
All around the ground was thirsty
In the preauroral cool.
    Dewfall drenched the Judge's fleece;
    Mary bears the Prince of Peace.

Lo the dreaming King of Babel
Saw a rock uncut by hand
Pulverize the banded idol,
Grow, and dominate the land.
   Jesus is that cornerstone,
   Now into a mountain grown.

Lo a branch grows out of Jesse;
Kings of Jewry are its wood.
Jesus is its bud and blossom,
Born to shed His royal blood.
   Wolves and lambs together dwell;
   Mary bears Emmanuel.

A CARRACK AND TWO CARAVELS
A CAROL FOR ADVENT

King David and the Sibyl wait
On facing brinks across a strait.
Each watches from a chalky clift.
Three ships approach them, sailing swift.

A caravel, all rigged in blue,
Has white-clad angels for its crew.
A blue-clad Lady kneels aboard;
It bears the bearer of the Lord.

A second comes. There kneels inside
A Prophet girt in camel hide.
Its sails are dyed in virid hues.
It bears the bearer of the News.

A carrack comes. Its sails are red,
Like dress of vintners as they tread.
Saint Michael at its tiller stands.
He steers the ship with steady hands.

Saint Gabriel with silver horn
Stands at its bow from morn to morn.
The trumpet at the angel's lips
Sounds from the bravest of the ships.

Its sails are red as blood and wine.
Its masts are fir and box and pine.
A red-robed Doomsman sits within;
It bears the Bearer of our sin.

Three ships advance between the scarps.
Their angel crews are playing harps.
King David and the Sibyl sing;
They laud the burdens that they bring.

A carrack and two caravels:
Their angel crews are ringing bells.
The morning sun illumines them
As they advance to Bethlehem.

THE DEW FALLS
A HYMN FOR ADVENT

The dew falls on the dusty soil
That wheat may come, and wine, and oil.
The rain of justice, after drought,
Arrives to make a Savior sprout.
    Behold the liquor from the sky
    That Jesus Christ is gotten by.

A maiden in a wooded place
Hears hounds and hunters giving chase.
Their quarry sprints, evades the trap,
And rests its head upon her lap.
    The noblest beast of mother born
    Is Jesus Christ the unicorn.

The planets and the stars appear
To mark the season, day, and year.
They luminate the murky earth
And indicate a time for birth.
    The welkin's brightest light by far
    Is Jesus Christ the Morning Star.

The stone the builders cast aside
Is lovingkindness petrified.
It is as fulgent and as hard
As polished jasper, polished sard.
   The choicest gem the earth has known
   Is Jesus Christ the arkenstone.

The thorn and lily, wheat and tare
A scatter-seeded garden share.
And so together they shall bloom
Until the harvest day of doom.
   The final judge of all that grows
   Is Jesus Christ the Golden Rose.

THE FRUIT OF THY WOMB
A HYMN FOR ADVENT

The fruit of the tree is delightful to see;
It has been so since Eve picked the plum.
But birth-pangs and toil in the thistle-thick soil
Were the consequent curses therefrom.

The fruit of the field is a nourishing yield;
It has been so since Cain cut his corn.
But he who sowed seeds did the foulest of deeds
And spilled blood of his brother next-born.

The fruit of the vine is the gladdening wine;
It has been so since Noah trod must.
But nakedness, shame, and contumely came
To the patriarch blameless and just.

Hail Mary! Thou bearest the unblemished pear:
Not the pear whereby Eve was enticed,
Not the wild pear of Nod, but the gustable God:
Yea, the fruit of thy womb, Jesus Christ.

The fruit of thy womb is the Bread of Life whom
All the hungry repentant will eat.
No natural grain can so wholly sustain
As God's flesh guised as azymes of wheat.

The fruit of thy Womb is the offering whom
All the thirsty repentant will taste.
This liquid divine is God's blood guised as wine,
Poured to ransom the low and disgraced.

This first-born of creature, this unblemished peach,
Hangs alone on the Tree of Life's limb.
Peeled, pitted, and sliced, He is God sacrificed;
Lo a curative juice flows from Him.

Hail Mary! With thee God has humbled to be;
Human flesh, human blood to assume.
No fruit of the earth has so glorious worth
As the quickening fruit of thy womb.

WHEN GOD MADE ADAM
A HYMN FOR CHRISTMAS AT MIDNIGHT

When God made Adam from the earth,
He gave him airy breath.
   A heart like fire burned in the man.
   His humors like four rivers ran.
All elements were in his birth;
He was no slave to death.

When God made Adam from the slime,
He breathed into his face.
   The man became a living soul
   And harmony was in him whole.
He was no slave to passing time,
Nor to estranging space.

When Adam named the beasts and birds,
His voice as music rang:
   A voice so resonant and pure
   No sinful creature might endure
Its sound, nor understand the words
That sinless Adam sang.

When Adam fell, the fiends of Hell
Released their dismal screams.
   To laborers amid their riot,
   The songs of Paradise are quiet,
Like echoes from a distant bell,
Like half-remembered dreams.

And yet when Jubal struck his chime
And played his harp and flute;
   When David lauded God at morn
   With timbrel, psaltery, and horn;
Demonic noise was for a time
Unthreatening and mute.

And once when shepherds piped to sheep
The angels sang reply:
   Let rivers clap and hills rejoice;
   Ye mortal men, lift up your voice.
The second Adam lies asleep
To Mary's lullaby.

Go to His manger without fear;
Before the baby, bow.
   Behold the breaker of your chains
   To sin, to death, to endless pains.
Behold the ever-present Here,
The ever-present Now.

GOOD SHEPHERDS
A CAROL FOR CHRISTMAS AT MIDNIGHT

Righteous Abel was a shepherd;
He rebutted wolf and leopard.
   Shepherds, in the field abiding,
   Harken to the angel's tiding.
   Go to meet the God of Abel;
   He reposes in yon stable.

Jacob, who beheld the Ladder,
Guarded sheep from asp and adder.
   Shepherds quaking, greatly fearing,
   Heed the message ye are hearing.
   Go to see the Ladder's summit
   And the blessings flowing from it.

Moses, who confronted Pharaoh,
Guided flocks through fold-gates narrow.
   See the twelve angelic legions
   Winging through the starry regions.
   Go to meet the God of Moses;
   In yon stable He reposes.

David, christened King of Zion,
Rescued sheep from bear and lion.
 From the hills where David tended,
 Go to Bethlehem the splendid.
 Go to meet the God of David;
 All good shepherds shall be saved.

A LIGHT SHINES TODAY
A BALLADE FOR CHRISTMAS AT DAYBREAK

O nata lux de lumine,
Shine on this vale of gruesome gloom!
The night is past; now dawns the day
When mercy triumphs over doom.
Among the bramblebushes bloom
The lily and the Sharon rose.
Productive is the Virgin's womb;
Lux fulget hodie super nos!

O Oriens, O Morning Star,
Shine on the Adversary's host
That challenged very God to war,
All echoing the damning boast.
The false light-bearer flees, exposed
Before true light that burns and glows.
The daybreak glories unopposed;
Lux fulget hodie super nos!

O splendor lucis æternæ,
Shine on us, Adam's progeny
Who blindly reach and grasp and stray;
Anoint our eyes that we may see.
O Sol Iustitiæ, veni!
Be overhead and ever close
To us who wish to walk with Thee.
Lux fulget hodie super nos!

THE WORD OF GOD
A CAROL FOR CHRISTMAS DAY

Verbum Dei Deo natum,
   He who spun the broad stellatum,
   Set in sequence day and night,
And gave to each its regent light,
Lies in a manger, swaddled tight.

Verbum Patris humanatur,
   He who parted sky from water,
   Held the four winds in His fist,
And wrapped the sea in clouds and mist,
Is by His Virgin Mother kissed.

Verbum caro factum est.
The God who founded east and west
And north and south and filled them all
With things that run and walk and crawl
Lies in a crowded cattle stall.

Verbum Patris mundo fulsit.
   He who made the world and rules it
   To its last age from its first,
And brings redemption to the cursed,
Is by His Virgin Mother nursed.

Puer nobis natus est.
The boy who sleeps at Mary's breast
Is He who rides, and strikes with swords
The seven-headed monster's hordes:
The King of kings and Lord of lords.

PURPLE AND PALL
A BALLAD ON THE ARA CÆLI

Cæsar Augustus wore purple and pall.
His empire extended from Egypt to Gaul.
His empire extended from Jewry to Spain.
The world was at peace in the days of his reign.

Cæsar Augustus had silver and gold.
His subjects were everywhere taxed and enrolled.
He sat on his throne with an orb and a rod.
His senators wished to declare him a god.

Cæsar Augustus drank white wine and red.
His enemies either were banished or dead.
He sat on his throne and collected his tax
And felt his mortality creepingly wax.

Summon the Sibyl, his senators said,
To speak with the voice of the gods overhead.
And they will declare, we are certain, that thou
Belongest among them; pray summon her now.

Cæsar consented. The Sibyl appeared.
They stood on a hill and he bade her to weird.
They stood on the hill where
    the money was made.
The goddess of money
    was nearby displayed.

Tell, O Albunea, canst thou foresee
A victor or ruler more godly than me?
A master of legions more mighty in war?
A pontiff more worthy the lifeblood to pour?

Moving as though in a slumbery trance,
The Sibyl Albunea started to dance.
The Sibyl Albunea danced unawoke.
She suddenly looked to the heavens and spoke:

Harken, O Cæsar, to what I descry!
The sun at the peak of the midwinter sky
Has compassed about it a rainbow. Behold;
Its focus is He whom the Nine Books foretold.

Cæsar regarded, as though through a glass,
A boy in a stall with an ox and an ass.
A travel-worn maid took the boy on her lap;
She sang to her son and she offered her pap.

This is the Altar of Heaven thou seest.
The boy is thy sovran and prophet and priest.
His empire is endless. His subjects are free.
Behold Him, the emperor greater than thee.

Cæsar burned incense
    and offered a prayer.
Together they worshipped,
    he and the sooth-sayer.
The man-God and God-man was born in a stall
When Cæsar Augustus wore purple and pall.

THE VIRGIN SANG
A CHRISTMAS LULLABY

The Virgin sang: *Lulay, lulee,*
My son, my son, what dost Thou see?
   She kissed His cheek and held His hands,
   And bound Him tight in swaddling bands.
     I will be by a traitor kissed,
     And bound in ropes about the wrist.

The Virgin sang: *Balu, lalow,*
My son, my son, what dost Thou know?
   She stroked His features small and fair,
   And ran her fingers through His hair.
     I will be spat upon by liars,
     And mockingly be crowned with briars.

The Virgin sang: *Lulee, lulay,*
My son, my son, what wilt Thou say?
   She fed the infant at her breast,
   And laid Him in the hay to rest.
     I thirstily for drink will call,
     But vinegar be fed, and gall.

The Virgin sang: *Lalow, balu,*
My son, my son, what wilt Thou do?
   She knelt beside His manger bed,
   And for His safety prayed and pled.
     I will be punctured by a spear,
     With thou, My mother, standing near.

The Virgin sang: *Lulay, lulee,*
My son, my son, what wilt Thou be?
   She watched and wondered through the night,
   By moon and star and candle-light.
     I will be slain; I will be tombed;
     I will descend among the doomed.

The Virgin sang: *Balu, lalow,*
My son, my son, where wilt Thou go?
   She watched and wondered until dawn,
   Until the moon and stars were gone.
     I will awake; I will arise;
     I will ascend above the skies.

SING NOWELL
A CAROL FOR CHRISTMASTIDE

Shepherds, pipers, paupers come;
Bring a torch and bring a drum.
Merrymakers,
Fear-forsakers,
Leave your muttons in the acres.
   Sing Nowell, now is well,
   Sing anew, Alleluia.

Mysteries are in the spheres;
Chase the planet that appears.
Astromancers,
Find your answers.
Come as singers, come as dancers.
   Sing Io, gone is woe,
   Come and go, Alleluia.

Sinnermen from many lands,
Come with nothing in your hands.
At the manger,
Meet no danger;
Meet the King who loves the stranger.
  Sing amain, sing again,
  Sing Amen, Alleluia.

NEW YEARS AND AGES
A CAROL FOR CIRCUMCISION DAY

Cisio Ianus. Mirabilis annus.
New years and ages are dawning upon us.
Jesus has suffered for Abraham's token,
Shedding His blood for a promise unbroken.

Annus mirabilis. Cisio Ianus.
Angels are singing Amens and Hosannas.
Jesus will suffer for Adam's offending,
Shedding His blood for a promise unending.

Cisio Ianus. Mirabilis annus.
New years and ages are dawning upon us;
New revelations and new dispensations,
New testaments for all races and nations.

Filius genitus. Filius bonus.
Jesus will fashion our bodily lowness
Into the like of His glory exceeding:
Nevermore hurting and nevermore bleeding.

Filius genitus. Filius bonus.
Angels are singing a song multisonous.
New years and ages are dawning upon us.
Annus mirabilis. Cisio Ianus.

THE WISEST OF THE WISE
A HYMN FOR EPIPHANY

There lived in Tarshish clever men
    with eyes uncommon keen.
On cloudless nights they counted lights
    and mapped what they had seen.
They foretold plagues and famines by
    the comets and the stars.
They read the course of nations in
    the wanderings of Mars.
The wisest of their wise beheld
    the sky above the sea;
He saw a star that shone afar
    where no star ought to be.

The clever men of Araby
    were clever to a fault.
They pounded in their mortars brim-
    stone, mercury, and salt.
They read the Graven Emerald
    for secrets of the dead

To conjure immortality,
>   to conjure gold from lead.
The wisest of their wise beheld
>   the firmament across;
He saw a sun among the dark,
>   like gold among the dross.

There lived in Sheba clever men
>   with recollections vast.
They dug for things their queens and kings
>   had lost in ages past.
They sought the Ring of Solomon
>   that bound the fiends in thrall
And bade them quarry boulders for
>   the holy Temple's wall.
The wisest of their wise beheld
>   the sky above the sand;
He saw a star that beckoned him
>   to Solomon's own land.

The wisest men to Bethlehem
    made haste to offer gifts.
For them who seek, a baby meek
    unites what folly rifts.
A mine of providence divine
    in every nation hides.
For humble minds, a baby binds
    what ignorance divides.
The baby is the Light of lights;
    the baby is the Stone.
The baby is the King of kings;
    a manger is His throne.

THE TREASURES OF THE EARTH
A HYMN FOR EPIPHANY

What shall we bring to please a king?
    The treasures of the groves?
The tears of myrrh, the spikenard pure,
    the cardamom and cloves?
The calamus and cinnamon,
    the frankincense and gum?
The storied balm of Gilead,
    the Libyc silphium?

Bring what ye will, but not until
    your spirits be contrite.
No spicery of wort or tree
    is worth to Him a mite
Unless your hearts be broken like
    the kernel undertrod.
Do justly and love mercy and
    walk humbly with your God.

What shall we bring to please a king?
    The treasures of the seas?
The pearls as large as hazel-nuts,
    the tortuce panoplies?
The ambergrease, the golden fleece
    of pen-clams spun to silk?
The dyes of Africa and Tyre,
    squeezed from the lowly whilk?

Bring what ye will, but not until
    your spirits be contrite.
No adder's tongue on coral hung
    is worth to Him a mite
Unless your hearts be like the fish-
    es swimming in the flood
That issues from the Temple's side,
    of water and of blood.

What shall we bring to please a king?
    The treasures of the mines?
The adamant and emerald,
    the carbuncle that shines?
The hyacinth and amethyst,
    the liver-colored brass?
The orichalc, the kohl and talc,
    the gold and flexile glass?

Bring what ye will, but not until
    your spirits be contrite.
No glistering or gleaming thing
    is worth to Him a mite
Unless your hearts be softened in
    the dread Refiner's fire.
Be purified of damning pride,
    of luxury and ire.

What shall we bring to please a king?
　　　The treasures of the chase?
The pungent musks, the massive tusks
　　　sawn from a snouted face?
The winter coats of squirrels and stoats,
　　　the lettices and vairs?
The hooves and horns of unicorns,
　　　the skins of polar bears?

Bring what ye will, but not until
　　　your spirits be contrite.
No pelt or plume, no rare perfume
　　　is worth to Him a mite
Unless your hearts be simple and
　　　as harmless as the dove.
Be meek and poor. Your God adore.
　　　Your every neighbor love.

JESUS LIVES IN EGYPT
A CAROL ON THE FLIGHT INTO EGYPT

Herod in Jerusalem,
Pretender king to sons of Shem,
Sends murderers to Bethlehem;
Jesus lives in Egypt.
    Quia puer Israël, dilexi eum.
    Ex Ægypto vocavi filium meum.

Hid amid the sons of Cham,
A buried seed of Abraham,
A yearling kid, a spotless lamb,
Jesus lives in Egypt.
    Quia puer Israël &c

Hermes crumbles into dust,
As weak as iron consumed by rust.
With Mary mild and Joseph just,
Jesus lives in Egypt.
    Quia puer Israël &c

From his pillar tumbles Thoth,
As weak as wool consumed by moth.
A fugitive from Herod wroth,
Jesus lives in Egypt.
   Quia puer Israël tc

By the pharaonic tombs,
The broken-into, plundered rooms,
The palaces that sand inhumes,
Jesus lives in Egypt.
   Quia puer Israël tc

By the lunar shrines defiled,
With Joseph just and Mary mild,
A triply-great and holy child
Jesus lives in Egypt.
   Quia puer Israël tc

Tau is written on the wood,
The lintel marked with ovine blood.
Beneath this figure of the Rood,
Jesus lives in Egypt.
   Quia puer Israël tc

Aaron stretched his mighty Rod
Across this land; here Abram trod.
The rightful King, the lasting God,
Jesus lives in Egypt.
   Quia puer Israël, dilexi eum.
   Ex Ægypto vocavi filium meum.

THE WAY TO BETHLEHEM
A CAROL FOR EPIPHANYTIDE

What is the way to Bethlehem?
   Go as the planet guides.
Whom shall we find thereat enshrined?
   A king and a god besides.
If ye offer alms with no trumpet's blare,
Ye may come to the shed with whatever ye bear.
Ye may come to the shed,
    to the House of Bread;
A baby governs there.

Where do the waters of Jordan flow?
   Down to the Sea of Lot.
Can we be laved and can we be saved?
   None lives who yet cannot.
If ye wish to be buried and born anew,
Ye may come to the flood and be baptized too.
Ye may come to the flood
    where the fruit grows good;
The baptist waits for you.

Where is the wine for the wedding feast?
    Drunk to the very lees.
Must we thirst? Have the wineskins burst?
    Nay, there are more than these.
If ye do whatever the bridegroom says,
Ye may drink from His jars to the end of days.
Ye may drink from His jars;
    they are reservoirs
Of wine surpassing praise.

GOD IS IN THE TEMPLE AGAIN
A CAROL FOR CANDLEMAS

Climb the steps, O Mary the Virgin,
To the house of cedarwood gilt.
Bring thy son; His flesh is the Temple
That will be destroyed and rebuilt.

Bring the doves, O diligent Joseph,
As the Law of Moses requires.
Bring the boy; His Law will extinguish
Evermore the holocaust fires.

Spread thine arms, O Simeon, widely.
Death will tarry. Gladly adore,
See, and handle that consolation
Promised to the prophets of yore.

Sing thy song; the Spirit is in thee.
Bless and thank the Father divine.
Lift the Son, a light to the nations,
Over Jew and Gentile to shine.

Break thy fast, O Anna the widow.
Take thy rest; the Lord is awaked.
See true food and true drink before thee.
Live forever, sated and slaked.

Light a candle, join the procession,
O ye sons and daughters of men.
Purify your eyes and behold Him:
God is in the Temple again!

VANITAS VANITATUM
A SONG ON EARTHLY TRANSIENCE

Vanity, vanity, baubles and gauds.
The devil called Mammon has pedlars and bawds;
Their wares are whatever the worldling applauds.

Talents and time and attention and trust
Are wasted on treasures that molder and rust.
Remember, O man, thou art ashes and dust.

Castles and temples will crumble to rubble,
Flattened as low as the sickle-cut stubble;
Gone like a butterfly, gone like a bubble.

In icti oculi, fortune and fame
Are gone like a guttering candlestub's flame.
Remember, O man, thou art fragile of frame.

Ubi sunt principes? Ubi sunt reges?
Where are the worthies and where are the sages?
Gone like the snowfalls of earlier ages.

No man is spared for his wisdom or might,
His cunning or craft, his prophetical sight,
When Death like a pilferer comes in the night.

Gloria mundi will burn up like cotton:
Blindingly bright and then wholly forgotten.
Beauty will ripen and rapidly rotten.

No man is spared for his rank or renown,
His badges of honor, his crosier or crown,
When Death with his hunting-bow chases
    him down.

Nascendo morimur, babies and skulls.
Remember the angel who harvests and culls,
Who sharpens the scythe-blade no century dulls.

Vulnerant omnes, et ultima necat.
  What thou hast hoarded, prepare to forsake it.
    Man meets his Maker with nothing, and naked.
      Nude as though newborn, he will be awakened,
    Weighed by Saint Michael, and finally reckoned.
  Heed thou the horologe counting thy seconds,
Chiming a call to repentance that beckons.

IN THE DESERT
A CAROL ON THE TEMPTATION OF JESUS CHRIST

In the desert, Satan said:
    Turn the rubble into bread.
    Say the magic words and break
    Quarantine with Easter cake.
    Pandemonium will fain
    Feast with Thee on pandemain.

Jesus quoth the scripture known:
Man lives not by bread alone.
Every stone remained a stone.

On the steeple, Satan sneered:
    Everybody plucks the beard
    Of a god who cannot fly.
    We are better, Thou and I.
    Make the angels earn their keep,
    Burden-bearing them who leap.

Jesus quoth the scripture blest:
Put thy God not to the test.
Crowds below were unimpressed.

Satan shouted from the peak:
   Rule the Roman and the Greek!
   Rule as Pharaoh and as Khan
   Mexico and Babylon,
   Ind and Persia and Cathay.
   Bow to me, and homage pay.

Jesus quoth the Law once more:
God alone thou shalt adore.
Kings were kings as theretofore.

Get behind me and avaunt.
Trickery will not end want.
Trickery will not end doubt,
Bring eutopia about,
Or unlock the pearly gates.
Man will sorrow as he waits
Till I give the hidden bread,
Sit on clouds and judge the dead,
Cast down kings and rule instead.

MOUNT TABOR
A HYMN ON THE TRANSFIGURATION

Mount Carmel was scorched by the Deity's ire.
Mount Horeb was cloaked by
    His cloud and His fire.
Mount Nebo is fissured and pitted with caves
Where treasures of treasures
    are hidden, and graves.
Mount Tabor is favored more terribly still;
Theophany happens on top of this hill.

For here is Elijah, who rode in the car
With horses like torches, past planet and star;
Who high on a mountain contested belief
By calling down brimstone to burn up the beef.
Elijah, who will in the Antichrist's reign
Return to bear witness, and for it be slain.

And here too is Moses, with horns like a ram,
Who was the familiar of I Am Who Am;
Who high on a mountain His countenance saw,
And took from His hands the
    Commandments and Law;
Who died on a mountain and afterward hides,
His corse undisclosed while the old earth abides.

Between them is Jesus, His visage as bright
Compared to the sun as the sun to the night,
Yet causing no blindness, no blister or burn:
A face that anticipates glory eterne.
He holds conversation with friend and with friend,
Their Law and their Prophecy's ultimate end.

And here is Saint Peter, who sees the event,
And makes the proposal to build each a tent.
And here is a nimbus, and here is a voice.
*My Son and My dearworth, in whom I rejoice;
Attend Him!* the voice from the nimbus exclaims,
Astounding Saint Peter,
    Saint John, and Saint James.

Arise, ye who grovel, and be unafraid,
Says Jesus, who offers them comfort and aid.
Of what ye have seen here, let nothing be said
Until I have died and returned from the dead.
He climbs off the mountain and exits anon,
Ahead of Saint Peter, Saint James, and Saint John.

THE ANGEL'S GREETING
A CAROL ON THE ANNUNCIATION

The angel's greeting is strange; how sweetly
    the Virgin musters her courage at this!
Will truth and mercy forsooth embrace? And
    will peace and justice see reason to kiss?
To frightened persons in lightless places,
    the worthy Gabriel heralds the day;
The babe that Mary will birthe will carry
    alone our herited onus away.

Reversed is *Eva*; she hears the *Ave*. Not cursed
    but favored, she fears yet assents.
Behold the handmaid foretold in proverb,
    the Wisdom standing in Israël's tents.
Now Mary's body is Aaron's Rod bearing bloom
    and fruit, thaumaturgically greened.
Salute the Virgin whose womb has burgeoned!
    The Demiurge is no memberless fiend.

Come bring her daffodils; sing and laugh;
    put your quadragesimal penance aside.
Thank God who blesses a loving revel
    above a fast to feed splenitive pride!
Your feasts and levity cast out devils.
    Come masters; stoop to bucolical play.
Come priests and scholars to whoop and holler;
    no melancholer is welcome today!

MAIDEN WITHOUT DAPPLE
A CAROL ON THE ANNUNCIATION

Mary, maiden without dapple,
Said her psalter is a chapel.
Sudden as a thunderclap al-
it an angel, wings aflap.

Thou art favored! Do not fear it;
God shall wed thee to His Spirit,
Spake the angel in her ear.

In a woman without spot in
Her shall God by God be gotten.
Thine assent shall knit the knot.

Thou shalt flow with milk and melly,
Bearing in thy very belly
God-With-Us: Emmanuel. E-
mmanuel shall harrow Hell.

Call Him Jesus; He shall disem-
power him who rules Abysm,
Ending God and Adam's schism.
Kingship endless shall be His.

He shall rule the House of Jacob,
Pay the ransom for its sake, ob-
literate its bond, and break ab-
horrent contracts with the Snake.

He shall empty Satan's prison,
Rescue any wretch who is in-
side, and reigning truly risen,
Claim him once again as His.

Mary listened and assented
To a thing unprecedented.
Modestly, her knee she bent.

I shall be the ancillary
Of the Lord, responded Mary.
Gabriel took to the air.

Sunshine through a crystal prism,
Horns of consecrated chrism,
Rods ablossom, green and lissome,
Are less innocent than this.

THY BOSOM FRIEND
A CAROL ON THE BETRAYAL OF JESUS CHRIST

Mary, Mary, loose thy locks.
Break the alabaster box.
Tears and kisses freely give.
Balm the head and feet that live.
   Jesus is thy bosom friend;
   He will love thee to the end.

Mary, Mary, go in peace.
From thy debt thou hast release.
Heed not Judas's complaint;
Waste is worthy of a saint.
   Jesus is thy bosom friend;
   He will love thee to the end.

Judas, Judas, dip the bread.
Very soon thou wilt be dead:
Dead and hanging on a tree.
Thy friend Jesus, so will He.
   Jesus is thy bosom friend;
   He will love thee to the end.

Judas, Judas, plant the kiss.
Know that torment follows this.
Inwit gnawing like a beast,
Throw the money at the priest.
    Jesus is thy bosom friend;
    He will love thee to the end.

Peter, Peter, warm thy hands.
Hear the questions and demands.
Thy friend Jesus stands at trial,
Answering without denial.
    Jesus is thy bosom friend;
    He will love thee to the end.

Peter, Peter, curse and swear.
See thy friend and meet His stare.
At the crowing of the cock,
Tears flow from the stricken Rock.
    Jesus is thy bosom friend;
    He will love thee to the end.

COME WAVING BRANCHES
A CAROL FOR PALM SUNDAY

Come waving branches of olive and palm,
Singing a verse of your favorite psalm.
Lay down the garments and blankets ye bring
To welcome the ass and the colt and the King.

Come from the temple and come from the house,
Singing *Hosanna* and *Gloria laus*.
Play on your trumpets and timbrels and lutes
To welcome the King who is riding the brutes.

Come waving branches of sallow and yew,
Carrying baskets of petals to strew.
Climb up the sycamores; watch as they pass:
The Scion of David, the colt, and the ass.

Come all ye poor and ye halt and ye blind,
Leaving the unready fig-tree behind.
Fill the environs with music and cheers
To welcome the King of the Jews as He nears.

Come waving branches of laurel and box.
Lower the drawbridge; put keys in the locks;
Lift up the portcluse; unfasten the bolt
To welcome the King and the ass and the colt.

Come all ye halt and ye blind and ye poor.
Whoop as He knocks at the Merciful Door.
Hear ye His voice and invite Him to dine,
To share at your table the bread and the wine.

Come, ye Jerusalemites, in a throng;
Join with the angels and children in song.
Whoop as He opens the door and goes through:
The King who is riding a jument or two.

Come all ye blind and ye poor and ye halt;
Be as the light of the earth, and the salt.
Shout *Benedictus qui venit* amain
To welcome the King who is come to be slain.

BAKÈD BREAD AND WINE SO RED
A CAROL FOR MAUNDY THURSDAY

Recline at meat with Me and eat,
Said Jesus to His friends:
Bring wine so red and water wan,
Bring bread of wheat and bread of bran,
And learn what it portends.

I soon shall spill upon the hill
A flood of wan and red;
Of Noah's wine and Adam's ale,
Not from a bucket, laced with dwale,
But from My body dead.

The gushing flood, it is My blood:
The best wine saved for last.
The water is a bath to cleanse
Your sins; it drowns Creation's ends
In seas of mercy vast.

Bring bakèd bread and wine so red,
A paten and a cup.
Consume My heart; consume My reins;
Consume the lifeblood of My veins,
Rejoicing as ye sup.

Bring wine so red and bakèd bread,
A chalice and a plate.
Consume My spirit and My soul;
Consume My very Godhead whole,
Then ponder what ye ate.

With bread and wine and words of Mine,
This ritual repeat.
And love each other, I command:
Be not too masterly or grand
To wash each other's feet.

This maundy new I give to you,
Deputing you, My priests,
To keep the memory alive,
To break the bread, to unct and shrive,
To celebrate the feasts.

On love depends, My chosen friends,
All Prophecy and Law.
Now taste and see: the Lord is good;
His blood is drink; His flesh is food.
They tasted and they saw.

SING WELLAWAY
A CAROL ON THE AGONY IN THE GARDEN

The darkness falls on Olivet.
   Sing woe, sing wellaway, sing woe.
The darkness falls on Olivet.
His face is wet with crimson sweat.
   Sing woe, sing woe, sing wellaway.
   Quantæ sunt ipse tenebræ.

The beads of blood drip from His beard.
   Sing woe, sing wellaway, sing woe.
The beads of blood drip from His beard.
He is afeared to dree His weird.
   Sing woe, sing woe, sing wellaway.
   Timor mortis conturbat me.

The cup is lifted to His lips.
   Sing woe, sing woe, sing wellaway.
The cup is lifted to His lips.
He begs to sip not; then He sips.
   Sing woe, sing wellaway, sing woe.
   Quia amore langueo.

They come with bludgeons, blades, and brands.
   Sing woe, sing woe, sing wellaway.
They come with bludgeons, blades, and brands.
He bravely stands with empty hands.
   Sing woe, sing wellaway, sing woe.
   Fortis ut mors dilectio.

THE HEMLOCK
A CAROL ON THE DEATH OF JESUS CHRIST

The hemlock grows in springtime;
It grows among the stones.
When Jesus died on Calvary,
He watered Adam's bones.
   The setting of the sun and
   The coming of the gloom;
   The stripping of the altars and
   The silence of the tomb.

The hemlock bears a carrot
As lethal as a sword.
When Jesus died on Calvary,
His mother's heart was gored.
   The setting of the sun &c

The hemlock bears a kecksy
As hollow as a dearth.
When Jesus died on Calvary,
His passion broke the earth.
   The setting of the sun &c

The hemlock bears a parsley
As noxious as a pest.
When Jesus died on Calvary,
His blood ran north and west.
   The setting of the sun &c

The hemlock bears a blossom
As savage as a beast.
When Jesus died on Calvary,
His blood ran south and east.
   The setting of the sun &c

The hemlock grows in springtime;
It grows among the stones.
Good Jesus died on Calvary
On Parasceve at nones.
   The setting of the sun and
   The coming of the gloom;
   The stripping of the altars and
   The silence of the tomb.

A GODFORSAKEN GOD
AN ALPHABET ON THE DEATH OF JESUS CHRIST

Alone alone alone alone,
Behold, Christ suffers to *a*tone.

Behold His body thrashed by reeds.
Christ hangs upon the crux and *b*leeds.

Centurions and idle guards
Divide His garb by playing *c*ards.

Depending from the spattered rood,
Emmanuel is shivering, nu*d*e.

Each passerby casts in His teeth
Ferocious words of disbeli*ef*.

Forgetting prophecy and law,
Gnat-strainers scoff and utter *f*augh.

Gnat-strainers judge on God's behalf.
He cannot save Himself, they lau*gh*.

He hears them speak with tongues like fangs.
In silence, Jesus bleeds and *h*angs.

Justly sentenced thieves hang near.
Knave the first, behold him *j*eer.

Knave the second, hear him say:
Lord, have mercy, *k*yrie.

Lachrymosely, palm in palm,
Marys bring the bitter ba*l*m.

Many mock and malice them;
None does Jesus Christ conde*m*n.

Numbered are His ribs and chines:
Ones and fours and tens and *n*ines.

Onocrotals, unclean fowls,
Perch anigh with desert *o*wls.

Pilate writes. The priests, aback,
Question him about the *p*laque.

Queath the priests: Thou writest ill.
Reword the title with thy quill.

Rex et Anax, Christ incurs
Stigmata meant for treasoners.

Spat upon and cruelly cursed,
The King of Glory cries for thirst.

Toward His lips as dry as dust,
Ungracefully a sponge is thrust.

Vinegar and gall He sucks.
Xpist bleeds and hangs upon the crux.

X apostles hide themselves.
Ye see John's presence, not the xii's.

Ye see the Virgin's tears, and John's.
Ziz hides the sun; Leviathan yawns.

Ziz hides the moon; Behemoth pounds
& rages for the grisly zounds.

& now Christ Jesus hangs His head;
A godforsaken God is dead.

NO GREATER LOVE
A ROMANCE ON THE DEATH OF JESUS CHRIST

The overlords of Antioch
Advanced upon Bethzachary
With cavalry and battery
To subjugate the Maccabee.
They came with elephants of Ind
In glistering caparisons,
With onagers and scorpions
And mercenary garrisons.

The elephants were drunk upon
The blood of grape and mulberry,
Each brute a castle shouldering
To overlook the soldiery.
The tallest of the elephants
Wore heraldry of Eupator:
The blasphemer and murderer,
The worshipper of Jupiter.

Brave Eleazar Avaran
Ran underneath its abdomen.
Among its tread earth-shattering,
He stabbed again and stabbed again.
The elephant fell thund'rously,
Its turretry miscarrying,
Five hundred horsemen scattering,
Brave Eleazar burying.

❊ ❊ ❊

The Dorians were warriors,
The progeny of Hercules.
They sieged the towns of Attica,
Succeeding to encircle these.
The Pythoness had boldened them
With utterings predictory,
Declaring them invincible,
Assuring them of victory.

Unless, she said, ye dare to spill
The precious blood of royalty;
Of Codrus King of Attica,
The paragon of loyalty.
When Codrus learned the oracle,
He set aside his kingly crown.
In costume of a charcoaler,
From Athens he went singly down.

He went among the Dorians,
Insulting and misheeding them
Until they drew their swords and slew
The saintliest of heathendom.
But when by certain tokens his
Identity was verified,
The Dorians threw down their arms
And fled the country, terrified.

❋ ❋ ❋

When Jesus lived in Galilee,
The Sadducees and Pharisees
Attempted to entangle Him
In fallacies and heresies.
They murmured at His miracles,
His mercy and munificence.
He dared to touch the unclean man,
To cure him and forgive his sins.
He scandalized the Pharisees
With doctrine clear and luminant.
He put to shame their lack of blame,
Their paltry tithes of rue and mint.

The seventy-one elders of
Jerusalem were ill at ease,
For Jesus and His followers
Might kindle instabilities.
Their Roman overlords deplored
The bold and disobedient.
The High Priest Caiaphas advised
A sacrifice expedient:

One man shall die, lest ye and I
And all our nation be destroyed.
He ordered scribes to ready bribes
And temple guards to be deployed.

When Jesus kept His watch and wept
And sweated in Gethsemany,
They threatened Him with quarterstaves,
Like any common enemy.
The councilors and Caiaphas
Took perjury for evidence.
They sent Him to their overlords
For scourging, with malevolence.
They cried: *Let Him be crucified!*
And stirred the crowd to riotry,
Declaring to Tiberius
Their fealty's entirety.

❧ ❧ ❧

One man shall die, that ye and I
And sinners everywhere be spared;
That Jews at peace, and Rome and Greece,
May sing before the Chair prepared;
That all may sup and share the cup:
Barbarians, Samaritans,
And Ethiopes; that all may hope
For Abraham's inheritance.
Now Jesus cries His last and dies;
The bedrock hylomorphous rends.
No greater love has man than this:
To lay his life down for his friends.

A WRETCH ON A GALLOWS TREE
A SONG OF CONSOLATION

A wretch was hanged on a gallows tree,
With a robber to each side.
Who is he to me? murmured Dives to a Pharisee,
And it seemed the wretch replied:

I will be thy help in thy helplessness,
When thy fortunes rock and reel;
When the consolations of Lady Philosophy
Leave thee crushed beneath the Wheel.

I will be thy strength when thy flesh is weak,
When the light of thine eyes is dim,
When thy heart is melting like wax in thy viscera,
And thy limb pulls from thy limb.

I will moor thy mind in thy manic time,
Through its tempest and its blast,
When the fiend returns bringing
    seven confederates,
And thy worst state is the last.

I will fix thy faith when the heathen rage,
When the Law no more commands,
When the holy places are promised abominate
To the idols made by hands.

I will be thy meat when the harvest fails
And thy drink when the well runs dry;
When the foodgrain nourishes
    locusts and palmerworms
And thy babes in hunger cry.

I will guide thy way through the howling waste,
Where the thorns surround thy head;
Where the rose of Sharon is wilting and withering,
And the flourdelis is dead.

I will be thy friend in thy friendlessness,
When thy boon companions flee;
When the osculation of Judas Iscariot
Is the only kiss for thee.

I will take thy pain when thou liest slain,
When thy ghost and thy flesh repel;
I will take thy sorrow and want and anxiety
And relinquish them to Hell.

I will save thy soul, O thou Pharisee,
I will save thy soul, O Dives,
If ye put no trust in your
    riches and righteousness
At the finish of your lives.

BROKEN THINGS
A BALLAD FOR THE HOLY TRIDUUM

Good Moses broke the tablet stones;
Good Hezekiah broke the snake;
Good Jesus breaks the Bread of Life
For every sinner's sake.
   Attend, My friends, good Jesus says:
   A little while and I shall go.
   Ye shall be scandalized in Me
   Before the rooster's crow.

Good Hezekiah broke the snake;
Good Jeremiah broke the flask;
Good Jesus breaks a sweat and begs,
Besorrowed for His task.
   Awake, My friends, good Jesus says:
   A little I'm scared but yet not hurt.
   I'll but lie down and bleed awhile
   Upon the garden's dirt.

Good Jeremiah broke the flask;
False Hananiah broke the yoke;
Good Jesus breaks His stride and falls
Beneath a soldier's stroke.
   Weep not, My friends, good Jesus says;
   A little I'm hurt but yet not slain.
   I'll but lie down and bleed awhile,
   Then rise and walk again.

False Hananiah broke the yoke;
Good Moses broke the tablet stones;
Good Jesus breaks the Temple walls
Of His own flesh and bones.
   Keep faith, My friends, good Jesus says;
   A little I'm slain but yet not done.
   My soul will be in Hell awhile,
   Then rise with Easter's sun.

Good Moses broke the tablet stones;
Good Hezekiah broke the snake;
Good Jesus breaks the Gates of Hell,
Its captives to retake.
   Rejoice, My friends, good Jesus says
   To Adam, Abraham, and Eve:
   I come to trample sin and death.
   They climb the stairs and leave.

SEVEN TIMES SEVEN
A COUNTING SONG ON THE PASSION

Hickory dickory, barley and rye.
Count to seven and Jesus will die.
One for the silver that Judas took.
Two for the gold and the ledger book
Scattered as trash on the Temple floor.
Herod and Pilate are three and four.
Five for Persia, six for Greece,
Seven for Rome and the kingdoms cease.

Vintery mintery, medlars and pears.
God's in the garden, saying His prayers.
One for the agony, two for the cup.
Three and four for the crowd coming up.
Five for the man who is better not born.
Six for the ear that is bloodily shorn.
Seven for somebody naked who flees.
Vintery mintery, turnips and peas.

Hickory dickory, withy and spurge.
One for the pillar, two for the scourge.
Three for the crown of twisted thorn.
Four for the scarlet, five for the scorn.
Six for the spittle and seven, the blows
Pummeling God on His ears and His nose.
Who would dare such brutality do?
Hickory dickory, yarrow and rue.

Vintery mintery, madder and woad.
One for the rope, two for the goad.
Three for the hands that Simon lent.
Four for the women who weep and lament.
Five for the elders who snicker and scowl.
Six for Veronica holding her towel.
Seven for all of the dolorous way.
Vintery mintery, myrtle and bay.

Hickory dickory, cumin and dill.
One for the cranium under the hill.
Two for Mary, three for John.
Four for the gibbet that God's hanged on.
Five for the vinegar, six for the sponge.
Seven, Longinus who makes the lunge.
Water flows west and blood flows east;
Here is the wine for the wedding feast.

Vintery mintery, mushrooms and moss.
One for the laddertrip down from the Cross.
Mary and Mary and Mary make four.
Five for the jar from the spicery store.
Six for the Pharisee balming the corse,
Bearing it off by a cart and a horse.
Seven for Joseph who offers his tomb.
Vintery mintery, heather and broom.

Hickory dickory, parsley and chives.
Count to seven and Jesus revives.
One for the earthquake, two for the stone.
Three for the angel whose countenance shone.
Four for the napkin, five for the shroud.
Six and seven, the enemies cowed.
Who would dare such a wonder deny?
Hickory dickory, barley and rye.

FELIX CULPA
A CAROL FOR THE VIGIL OF EASTER

O happy fault! O happy fault!
The sin of Adam we exalt:
The necessary apple-bite
That led us to this blessèd night.

O blessèd night! O blessèd night!
We celebrate by candle-light
The resurrection of the Christ:
The Paschal Lamb we sacrificed.

O Paschal Lamb! O Paschal Lamb!
Our God would rather die than damn.
He gives His blood to mark the post
And lintel, and His flesh to roast.

O parted sea! O parted sea!
The exodus from slavery
That once was walked by Israël
Is walked by Adam out of Hell.

O Morning Star! O Morning Star!
On every point it bears a scar.
It rises from the broken door
Of Tartarus and sets no more.

O light of Christ! O light of Christ!
Our Parents are imparadised.
With seraphim they offer praise
And sing to greet the day of days.

O day of days! O day of days!
The morning's oriental rays
Disperse the shadows and the dread.
Our God is risen from the dead!

THE SIGN OF JONAH
A CAROL FOR EASTER

Listen, all ye generations wicked
    and misguided:
Jonah is the only portent unto
    you provided.
Mark the prophet incognito, fleeing
    like a coward,
Thrown into an ocean where the swells and
    billows towered.

    Jonah floundered in the sea.
    Tempest ceased, and thunderpeal.
    God's displeasure was revealed.
      Ecce signum Ionæ.

    Where the stillest waters were,
    Suddenly there was a whirl
    Sucking to a netherworld.
      Ecce signum Ionæ.

Dread Leviathan below
Gaped and swallowed Jonah whole.
Far above, the ocean rolled.
   Ecce signum Ionæ.

Day and day and welladay:
In the belly of a whale
Jonah hellishly was gaoled.
   Ecce signum Ionæ.

Rueful Jonah offered prayer:
*God, deliver me from peril.
I will go and be Thy herald.*
   Ecce signum Ionæ.

From the gorge and orcish maw
Jonah issued, bathed in gall,
Mother-naked, beardless, bald.
   Ecce signum Ionæ.

Vomited upon the shore,
Jonah grasped at sand and coral,
Mal-de-merish, seaweed-laurelled.
   Ecce signum Ionæ.

Breathing freely, seeing sky,
Jonah could not choose but smile,
Humble as a little child.
   Ecce signum Ionæ.

Even so the Son of Man shall three days
      be departed
Into Hell, to cut its bars and free the
      brokenhearted,
Bringing them up from corruption to His
      Temple's portals,
Giving joy to Jonah and to all cre-
      ated mortals.

CHRIST IS RISEN
A CAROL FOR EASTER

Mourning Martha, weeping Mary,
No more kindred shall ye bury.
Wear no more the weeds of sorrow.
Christ is risen with the morrow.

Sinking Peter, doubting Thomas,
Worrying despite the promise,
Keep your faith through these conjunctures.
Christ is risen; touch the punctures.

Hebrew Children, Paul and Silas,
Languishing in dungeons eyeless,
Tell the captives, slaves, and debtors:
Christ is risen; break your fetters!

Righteous Abraham and Sarah,
Waiting era after era,
Meet the kernel killed and buried.
Christ is risen; Hell is harried.

Righteous Noah, Job, and Daniel,
Meet the sprouted mustard granule.
See the Tree of Life extending.
Christ is risen; death is ending.

Light your lanterns, prudent virgins.
See the Tree of Life; it burgeons!
Taste its fruit and make thanksgiving;
Christ is risen and is living.

HE IS NOT DEAD
A CAROL FOR EASTER WEEK

He is not dead? A rumor spread,
A whispering, a wish,
A thing too strange to be believed,
Absurd and wizardish.

   I have seen Him like the gardener
   As I tarried in my grief.
   I have seen Him touch the cabbage plant
   And heal its trampled leaf.

He is not dead? A rumor spread,
A murmuring of hope,
A beacon light in sorrow's murk
For those who blindly grope.

   I have met Him on the way to town.
   I have heard the things He said.
   I have sat with Him, imbibing wine
   And eating broken bread.

He is not dead? A rumor spread,
Corroborated twice
By witnesses incapable
Of fraudulent device.

I have seen Him suck the honeycomb.
I have seen Him eat the fish.
I have seen Him wash the morsels down
And lick the oily dish.

He is not dead? A rumor spread,
A stammering for joy,
A thing no odium can quash,
No violence destroy.

I have met Him in the upper room
When the doors were barred and chained.
I have stuck my fingers in the hands
That iron pegs profaned.

He is not dead? A rumor spread,
A clamoring, a cry,
A purple dayspring in the east
That saturates the sky.

I have felt Him push me from my horse
When I kicked against the pricks.
I have felt the spear-thrust of His voice
My hardened heart transfix.

He is not dead? A rumor spread,
A trumpeting, a blast,
A thing to leave all enemies
Astounded and aghast.

We have seen the Lord; He is no ghost;
He is flesh and bone and breath.
He is sallying upon the earth,
The conqueror of death.

EVERY EWE AND RAM
A CAROL ON THE GOOD SHEPHERD

The Shepherd true
Knows every ewe
And ram in the flock He tends.
For any stray
Or runaway,
He will seek to the earthly ends.

The Shepherd good
Will scour the wood,
The moor and the mountain steep;
Not idly bide,
Being satisfied
With ninety-nine other sheep.

The Shepherd will not
Leave one forgot,
Nor rest till He gathers in
That wayward sheep
Sunk nostril-deep
In the horrible pit of sin.

That miry clay
Is cold and gray,
Though seemingly warm and bright.
The warmth it gives
Kills all that lives;
Its light turns day to night.

Ye sunken sheep
Who brux and weep
And bellow; do not despair.
Ye may yet rise
From the pit of lies,
For the Shepherd will find you there.

He will lift you out
Of the quag of doubt,
And carry you in His arms
From filthy pelf,
From pride of self,
From a million moral harms.

He will wash your wool
In waters cool,
And lead you to pastures fat,
To rest and graze
Unto length of days
On the greenery grown thereat.

ABUNDANT SIGNS AND WONDERS
A HYMN ON THE ASCENSION

Past the brook and olive orchard
Where He shook like someone tortured,
Jesus stands upon a summit
And commands His college from it.
Hark and hear Him, ye apostles:
Gather near like flocking throstles.
Christ exhorts with more importance
As His time among you shortens:

> Speak the tongue of every nation.
> Smear the unguent of salvation.
> Pour the sacramental waters
> Over mackled sons and daughters.
> Promise peoples peace and pardon.
> Feed My sheep and keep My garden.
> Shear the toison. Reap the foison.
> Swallow any deadly poison.

Handle asps and cockatrices.
Greet with clasps and holy kisses
Tax collectors, sinners, strangers;
Nought infects and nought endangers.
Where malevolence is housened,
Cast out devils by the thousand.
Build religiously My bridges.
Catch My fish in hauls prodigious.

Purge with hyssop all believers;
Sins shall disappear, and fevers.
Pray with bountiful devotion,
Ousting mountains to the ocean,
Making lazars whole and guerished,
Even raising up the perished.
Work abundant signs and wonders
Till I come with clouds and thunders.

Christ, His sermon having ended,
Through the firmament ascended
Unencumbered into Heaven,
Leaving dumbstruck the eleven.
Why stand staring, Galileans?
Join the seraphs, singing pæans.
Transitory is all worry;
Jesus will return in glory.

COME TO THE FEAST
A SONG FOR THE DOWNTRODDEN

Tatterdemalions, mendicants, aliens,
Vagabonds, wanderers, come to the feast!
Come from the edges of highways and hedges;
The last shall be first and the first shall have least.

Lepers, come ringing your handbells and singing;
Lead all who are stricken with cankers and hurts.
Madmen bedevilled, unclothed and dishevelled,
Come now to the hall to receive your deserts.

Drunkards and sinners, demanders for glimmer,
Ye pickpockets, abracadabrists, and cheats;
Squanderers, harlots in raiment of scarlet,
Be penitent somewhat and everyone eats!

Takers of taxes and headsmen with axes,
Be shunned nevermore; be not branded like Cain.
Leave off beheading and come to the wedding;
Find pardon and peace, and companions remain.

All ye disparaged, come now to the marriage.
Recline at the table, eat fatlings and beeves.
Don the white garment and fear no debarment;
This feast is the feast that no hungry man leaves.

FIDIS

A GLOSSARY OF UNUSUAL WORDS AND PHRASES

abracadabrist	A MAGICIAN OR TRICKSTER
adamant	THE HARDEST OF ALL STONES
Abysm	ABYSS OR HELL
Adam's ale	WATER (ALCOHOLIC BEVERAGES DID NOT EXIST UNTIL THEIR INVENTION BY NOAH)
adder's tongue	FOSSIL SHARK TEETH, MISTAKEN FOR THE TONGUES OF SNAKES, WERE ONCE BELIEVED TO DETECT POISON. THESE AMULETS WERE PRESENTED AT BANQUETS, HUNG ON A LITTLE TREE MADE FROM POLISHED RED CORAL
afeared	AFRAID
Albunea	THE TIBURTINE SIBYL, A PROPHETESS OF ANCIENT ROME

ambergrease	AMBERGRIS, A DIGESTIVE PRODUCT OF SPERM WHALES USED IN PERFUMERY
anax	GREEK WORD FOR A KING
Ara Cæli	THE ALTAR OF HEAVEN
arkenstone	A PRECIOUS GEM
astromancer	AN ASTROLOGER
azymes	UNLEAVENED BREAD
benedictus qui venit	BLESSED IS HE WHO COMES (IN THE NAME OF THE LORD)
besom	A BROOM. THE BESOM OF DESTRUCTION IS MENTIONED BY THE PROPHET ISAIAH
Brig of Dread	A BRIDGE TO PURGATORY CROSSED BY DEPARTED SOULS, NAMED IN THE LYKE-WAKE DIRGE. A BRIDGE OF ONE HAIR APPEARS IN THE FAIRY TALE MOLLY WHUPPIE
Bruin	A BEAR (AFTER A CHARACTER IN MEDIEVAL BEAST FABLES)
brux	TO GNASH TEETH
bucolical	RUSTIC

caravel	A SMALL SHIP USED IN THE AGE OF EXPLORATION
carbuncle	A SMOOTH, DARK RED GEM
carrack	A LARGE SHIP USED IN THE AGE OF EXPLORATION
Cathay	CHINA
chine	BACKBONE
cisio lanus	THE FIRST WORDS OF A MNEMONIC POEM FOR REMEMBERING THE DATES OF LITURGICAL FEASTS. CISIO REFERS TO THE CIRCUMCISION OF CHRIST, CELEBRATED ON JANUARY FIRST
Codrus	THE LAST KING OF ATHENS
corse	CORPSE
dance macaber	DANSE MACABRE, A MEDIEVAL ALLEGORY OF THE IMPARTIALITY OF DEATH, IN WHICH MEN OF EVERY SOCIAL RANK DANCE WITH MUMMIES OR SKELETONS REPRESENTING THEIR DEAD SELVES

dearworth	BELOVÈD
demander for glimmer	A BEGGAR MAKING FRAUDULENT CLAIMS OF BEING BURNED OUT OF HOUSE AND HOME
Demiurge	THE MAKER OF THE WORLD. ACCORDING TO THE GNOSTIC HERESY, THIS WAS AN EVIL BEING, SOMETIMES DEPICTED AS A LION-HEADED SERPENT
Dives	A WEALTHY MAN WHO IGNORES THE POOR
doom-scales	IN MEDIEVAL DEPICTIONS OF THE LAST JUDGMENT, EACH SOUL IS MEASURED IN A BALANCE HELD BY THE ARCHANGEL MICHAEL
doomsman	A JUDGE
dree his weird	TO SUBMIT TO HIS DESTINY
dwale	A SLEEPING DRAUGHT MADE FROM BELLADONNA
Ecce signum Ionæ	BEHOLD THE SIGN OF JONAH
eterne	ETERNAL

Eupator	THE SELEUCID EMPEROR ANTIOCHUS V
Ex Ægypto vocavi filium meum	OUT OF EGYPT I CALLED MY SON
faugh	AN EXCLAMATION OF CONTEMPT OR DISGUST
felix culpa	HAPPY FAULT
filius bonus	A GOOD SON
filius genitus	A BEGOTTEN SON
flexile glass	ACCORDING TO PLINY, A FLEXIBLE GLASS WAS INVENTED DURING THE REIGN OF TIBERIUS, BUT SUPPRESSED DUE TO CONCERN THAT IT WOULD DEVALUE GOLD AND SILVER
floresce	TO BEAR FLOWERS
flourdelis	FLEUR-DE-LIS, A LILY FLOWER
foison	HARVEST
foliate	TO GROW LEAVES
Fortis ut mors dilectio	LOVE IS AS STRONG AS DEATH
gaud	A TRINKET

gloria laus	GLORY, LAUD (AND HONOR TO THEE, REDEEMER KING)
gloria mundi	IN THE PAPAL CORONATION CEREMONY, FLAX WAS RITUALLY BURNED WHILE SIC TRANSIT GLORIA MUNDI WAS DECLARED: SO PASSES THE GLORY OF THE WORLD
goddess of money	JUNO MONETA, IN WHOSE TEMPLE ROMAN COINS WERE MINTED
golden fleece of pen-clams	BYSSUS, A SILK WOVEN FROM FILAMENTS SECRETED BY MEDITERRANEAN CLAMS
Golden Rose	A GOLD ORNAMENT IN THE SHAPE OF A ROSE WAS BLESSED BY POPES ON THE FOURTH SUNDAY OF LENT
Graven Emerald	THE SMARAGDINE TABLET, AN ALCHEMICAL TEXT ATTRIBUTED TO HERMES TRISMEGISTUS

guerished	HEALED
handbell	LEPERS WERE ONCE REQUIRED TO CARRY BELLS OR CLAPPERS TO WARN OTHERS OF THEIR APPROACH
heckle-pin moor	THE WHINNY MOOR, DESCRIBED IN THE LYKE-WAKE DIRGE, IS AN ORDEAL PASSED BY DEPARTED SOULS. THOSE WHO GAVE ALMS OF SHOES WHEN ALIVE RECEIVE SHOES TO PROTECT THEM FROM ITS THORNS. THE WELL OF THE WORLD'S END, A FAIRY TALE, MENTIONS A MOOR OVERGROWN WITH PLANTS WHOSE THORNS ARE HECKLE-PINS, THE SHARP TEETH OF COMBS USED TO PROCESS FLAX
herited	INHERITED
hill where the money was made	THE CAPITOLINE HILL, ONE OF THE SEVEN HILLS OF ROME

horns like a ram	AFTER MOSES RECEIVED THE TABLETS OF LAW THE SECOND TIME, HIS FACE WAS GLORIFIED. THE HEBREW WORD DESCRIBING IT LITERALLY SAYS THAT MOSES GREW HORNS. THE VULGATE PASSED ON TO MEDIEVAL ARTISTS THIS LITERAL INTERPRETATION
horologe	CLOCK
House of Bread	BETHLEHEM
housened	HOUSED
hylomorphous	HAVING MATTER AND FORM, IN THE ARISTOTELIAN SENSE
in icti oculi	IN THE BLINK OF AN EYE
Ind	INDIA
inhume	TO BURY
inwit	CONSCIENCE
Jewry	THE KINGDOM OF JUDAH
jument	A BEAST OF BURDEN
kecksy	THE HOLLOW STALK OF AN UMBELLIFEROUS PLANT

Lady Philosophy	A PERSONIFICATION FROM THE CONSOLATION OF PHILOSOPHY BY BOËTHIUS
lettice	THE WHITE WINTER FUR OF A SNOW WEASEL
Libyc	FROM NORTHERN AFRICA
liver-colored brass	HEPATIZON, A VALUABLE BRONZE IN ANCIENT GREECE
Lux fulget hodie super nos	A LIGHT SHINES UPON US TODAY
mackled	STAINED OR SINFUL
mal-de-merish	SEASICK
mappemond	MAPPA MUNDI, A MAP OF THE ENTIRE WORLD
maundy	COMMANDMENT
melancholer	PENSIVE SORROW
melly	HONEY
Merciful Door	THE EASTERN (GOLDEN) GATE OF THE TEMPLE MOUNT
mirabilis annus	YEAR OF WONDER
mother-naked, beardless, bald	MEDIEVAL ART OFTEN SHOWS JONAH EMERGING FROM THE FISH NAKED AND HAIRLESS

multisonous	POLYPHONIC
Nascendo morimur	AS WE ARE BORN, WE DIE. THE TITLE OF BAROQUE PAINTINGS DEPICTING BABIES PLAYING WITH SKULLS
Nine Books	A COLLECTION OF PROPHECIES PURCHSED FROM THE SIBYLS BY TARQUIN THE PROUD AND LATER CONSULTED BY EMPERORS IN TIMES OF CRISIS
nones	THE NINTH HOUR OF THE DAY, ABOUT THREE O'CLOCK IN THE AFTERNOON
O nata lux de lumine	O LIGHT BORN OF LIGHT
O Oriens	O EAST
O Sol Iustitiæ, veni	O SUN OF JUSTICE, COME
O splendor lucis æternæ	O SPLENDOR OF ETERNAL LIGHT
onager	A TORSION CATAPULT
onocrotal	PELICAN
orcish	CHARACTERISTIC OF A KILLER WHALE, AN OGRE, OR THE CHTHONIC DEITY ORCUS

orichalc	A REDDISH PRECIOUS METAL. ACCORDING TO PLATO'S CRITIAS, IT WAS ONCE MINED IN ATLANTIS
pandemain	PANIS DOMINI, WHITE BREAD FIT FOR A LORD
Pandemonium	ALL THE DEMONS
panoply	A SUIT OF ARMOR
Parasceve	FRIDAY, THE DAY OF PREPARATION BEFORE THE SABBATH
pelf	ILL-GOTTEN WEALTH
pontiff	A HIGH PRIEST OF ANCIENT ROME. FROM THE REIGN OF AUGUSTUS, THE EMPEROR HELD THE OFFICE OF PONTIFEX MAXIMUS
portcluse	PORTCULLIS
Puer nobis natus est	UNTO US A CHILD IS BORN
purple and pall	PRECIOUS DYED CLOTH
Pythoness	THE ORACLE AT DELPHI
Quantæ sunt ipse tenebræ	HOW GREAT IS THAT DARKNESS
quadragesimal	LENTEN

quarantine	A FAST LASTING FORTY DAYS. THE PLACE WHERE CHRIST WAS TEMPTED IS CALLED MOUNT QUARANTINE
queath	TO SAY
Quia amore langueo	BECAUSE I LANGUISH FOR LOVE
Quia puer Israël, dilexi eum	BECAUSE ISRAËL WAS A CHILD, I LOVED HIM
reins	KIDNEYS, SUPPOSEDLY THE SEAT OF DESIRES
rex	LATIN WORD FOR A KING
Reynard	A FOX (AFTER A CHARACTER IN MEDIEVAL BEAST FABLES)
Ring of Solomon	ACCORDING TO CERTAIN LEGENDS, THE SIGNET RING OF SOLOMON GRANTED HIM POWER OVER BOTH GOOD AND EVIL SPIRITS
scorpion	A SIEGE ENGINE RESEMBLING A LARGE CROSSBOW
Sibyl	A PROPHETESS OF ANCIENT GREECE OR ROME

silphium	AN HERB USED IN ANCIENT COOKERY AND MEDICINE, PROBABLY EXTINCT
Slough of Despond	A SWAMP DESCRIBED IN THE PILGRIM'S PROGRESS, SIGNIFYING A STATE OF DESPAIR
sovran	SOVEREIGN
splenitive	SPLENETIC, BAD-TEMPERED
stellatum	THE CELESTIAL SPHERE OF THE FIXED STARS
tatterdemalion	A SHABBILY-CLOTHED PERSON
Tau is written	MEDIEVAL ART OFTEN SHOWS THE BLOOD OF THE PASCHAL LAMB PAINTED IN THE SHAPE OF A LETTER T ON THE ISRAËLITES' DOORPOSTS
tears of myrrh	ACCORDING TO OVID, MYRRHA WAS TURNED INTO A TREE AS PUNISHMENT FOR INCEST. ITS AROMATIC SAP REPRESENTS HER TEARS
thaumaturgically	MIRACULOUSLY
throstle	SONG THRUSH

Timor mortis conturbat me	THE FEAR OF DEATH TROUBLES ME
toison	FLEECE
tortuce	TORTOISE. THIS WORD ONCE DESCRIBED ALL TESTUDINES, MARINE OR TERRESTRIAL
Ubi sunt principes?	WHERE ARE THE PRINCES?
Ubi sunt reges?	WHERE ARE THE KINGS?
unct	TO ANOINT
vair	SQUIRREL FUR ARRANGED IN A PATTERN THAT ALTERNATES THE GRAY BACKS AND WHITE BELLIES
vanitas vanitatum	VANITY OF VANITIES (ALL IS VANITY)
Verbum caro factum est	THE WORD WAS MADE FLESH
Verbum Dei Deo natum	THE WORD OF GOD, BORN OF GOD
Verbum Patris humanatur	THE WORD OF THE FATHER MADE MAN
Verbum Patris mundo fulsit	THE WORD OF THE FATHER SHONE UPON THE WORLD

Vulnerant omnes, et ultima necat	EVERY (HOUR) WOUNDS, AND THE LAST ONE KILLS. A TRADITIONAL INSCRIPTION ON CLOCKS AND SUNDIALS
weird	TO PROPHESY
welkin	SKY OR HEAVEN
Wheel	THE ROTA FORTUNÆ, AN ANCIENT SYMBOL OF THE VAGARIES OF FORTUNE
whilk	WHELK. SEA SNAILS WERE THE SOURCE OF AN EXPENSIVE PURPLE DYE
Xpist	THE FIRST LETTERS OF THE NAME CHRIST WERE SOMETIMES WRITTEN IN GREEK CHARACTERS, CHI AND RHO
Ziz	A GIANT BIRD, RESEMBLING A GRIFFIN, WITH WINGS WIDE ENOUGH TO VEIL THE SUN
zounds	GOD'S WOUNDS
&	THE AMPERSAND WAS ONCE CONSIDERED THE FINAL LETTER OF THE LATIN ALPHABET

A NOTE ON THE TYPE

The typefaces used in this book were designed by Daniel Mitsui. These are:

Benedict, a Gotico-Antiqua;

Michaëla, its Italic companion;

ADAM, A SANS-SERIF;

and a set of Lombardic display capitals named

.

www.ingramcontent.com/pod-product-compliance
Lightning Source LLC
Chambersburg PA
CBHW031137090426
42738CB00008B/1130